CLOSER...
CLOSER...

!

NEVER CHASE
A PIPER CUB.

7-13

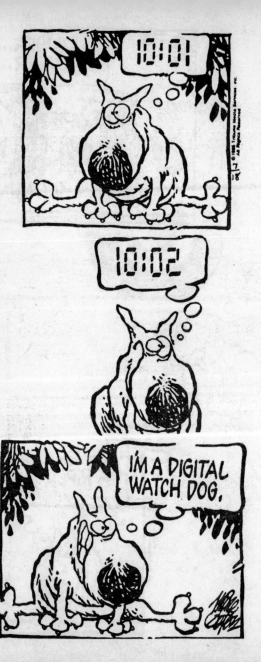

MIKE PETERS 8-15

FIZZT FIZZT...

true...

9-13

STRANGE.. I'VE GOT BUTTERFLIES IN MY STOMACH...

..IT MUST HAVE BEEN THAT CATERPILLAR I ATE.

ZIP

12-7

SPRONG....

THAT COLD, HUH?...

THAT COLD.

ONE YEAR TO A MAN IS SEVEN YEARS TO A DOG.

3-8

HMMM, ULP...

IN FOUR YEARS I'LL BE ON MEDICARE.

ATTENTION, I NEED SOME ATTENTION...